A·Z·T·E·C
ASTROLOGY

A·Z·T·E·C ASTROLOGY

·

An Introduction

MICHAEL COLMER

Illustrated by Peter Komarnyckyji

BLANDFORD

A BLANDFORD BOOK

First published in the UK 1995 by Blandford
A Cassell Imprint
Cassell plc, Wellington House
125 Strand, London WC2R 0BB

Distributed in the United States by
Sterling Publishing Co., Inc.
387 Park Avenue South, New York, NY 10016—8810

Distributed in Australia by
Capricorn Link (Australia) Pty Ltd
2/13 Carrington Road, Castle Hill, NSW 2154

British Library Cataloguing-in-Publication Data
A catalogue record for this book is available from the
British Library

ISBN 0–7137–2455–2

Typeset by Litho Link Ltd, Welshpool, Powys, Wales
Printed and bound in Finland by Werner Söderström Oy

Contents

—————•—————

You tell me then that I must perish
like the flowers that I cherish.
Nothing remains of my name,
nothing remembered of my fame?
But the gardens I planted still are young —
the songs I sang will still be sung.

Huéxotzin, Prince of Texcóco, c. 1484

Preface

————————————•————————————

WELCOME to the fascinating world of Aztec astrology – a science sadly neglected by astrologists for too long.

As each month passes and yet another temple, tomb or ziggurat (sacred astrological observatory) is uncovered in the jungles of Central America, so too are snippets which add further pieces to the jigsaw of this once-proud civilization and the way it interpreted star-gazing in its daily routine. Thanks to the persecution by the fanatical padres who accompanied those sixteenth-century conquistadores, the jigsaw remains frustratingly patchy, but more details get added to it every year.

I've taken the sum of our present knowledge and applied it to thousands of famous (and infamous) people to reach a modern interpretation of Aztec astrology. The results of this research appear in the pages that follow and offer astonishing insights into the human condition.

At first, it may seem odd to think of ourselves not as a Scorpio – or any other familar Western zodiac sign – but as Wind or Alligator or Flower. However, combine Western and Aztec astrology and we might just possibly discover more about how we tick, our potential (and potential pitfalls).

Much more work is needed before we can fully understand this fascinating 'new' system of applying the subtle energies of heavenly bodies to our human sensitivities.

Nevertheless, l hope this book will serve as an incentive to trigger other astrologists to take up their ephemerides in search of knowledge.

Finally, please note that Peter Komarnyckyji's illustrations are based on traditional Aztec designs and motifs.

A
Brief History of
the Aztecs

———————•———————

Some say they were refugees from the lost continent of
Atlantis; others believe they originated from the Ten Lost
Tribes of Israel. Whatever their origins, they came from Asia
to the Americas across the land-bridge now submerged by the
Bering Straits — 20,000 years before the birth of Christ. They
wandered down through North America to settle in what is
now called MesoAmerica, land that was later to be divided
into Mexico, Guatemala, Honduras, Belize and El Salvador.

By 2,500 BC they were cultivating *Zea mays* (corn) and
beginning to establish well-planned cities, with networks of
canals, in which commerce thrived. (This was at a time when
Egypt had just built its first pyramid and England was
constructing its famous stone circles, like the one at Avebury
in Wiltshire; the neighbouring one at Stonehenge was
erected much later.)

Between AD 250 and 900, these Mayans had mastered
mathematics, perfected the most complex system of writing
glyphs and created astrological calendars so accurate that
they can pinpoint any one day in 370,000 years!

As their civilization prospered, so it changed; as did the
Mayans' name: they begat the Olmecs, the Zapotecs, Nazcas,
Mochicas, Toltecs, Mixtecs and, finally, the Aztecs.

Then came the fifteenth century and explorers like
Christopher Columbus. In his wake came the gold-lusting
conquistadores, accompanied by fanatical priests determined
to convert the 'heathen'. These zealous priests ordered all
Mayan literature to be burned. So thorough and ruthless were
they that today only four of their sacred bark-paper books
remain: it was cultural genocide.

Accumulated Aztec gold of centuries was pillaged and
shipped back to Spain to form the basis of today's Western
economies (some being 'diverted' by Queen Elizabeth 1's
favoured privateers to English coffers).

All that is left of this very advanced civilization is an
incredible collection of temples, tombs and ziggurats, and a
whole lot of mystery. So it's hardly surprising that this region
has become the hottest property in archaeology today.

One of the few remaining clues to this civilization lies in
the work of the Catholic Bishop Diego de Landa, whose book
Relación de las Cosas de Yucatán gives an account of Mayan
culture. However, it was not until 1839, when the Anglo-
American writer/artist team of Stephens and Catherwood
fought their way through the Central American rain forests to
rediscover the ruins of Copan, Palenque and Uxmal, that
popular interest began.

Fifty years later, British explorer Alfred Maudsley began
cataloguing Mayan buildings. Then the excavations began.
One hundred years later, it was the turn of Washington's
Carnegie Institution archaeologists, Eric Thompson and
Sylvanus Morley. Ever since, this unusual and persecuted
culture intermittently surrenders yet another clue to its past.

One modern archaeologist, Tennessee University's
Arthur Demerest, recently explained this fascination to *Time*
magazine: 'You've got lost cities in the jungle, secret
inscriptions that only a few can read, tombs with mysteries in
them and the mystery of why it all collapsed.'

Today, more and more tourists are hitting the Aztec trail

to see for themselves what all this excitement is about. And with them comes this fascination with this ancient and mysterious culture.

Few realize that there are Mayans still around: an estimated 1.2 million live in the southern Mexican state of Chiapas and a further 5 million survive in the Yucatan Peninsula and in the rural communities of Belize, Guatemala, Honduras and El Salvador.

For an all-but-forgotten race with a highly sophisticated history, their plight is not a happy one. Centuries of persecution and cultural isolation have turned these people into outcasts in their own lands. Amnesty International is deeply concerned about the suffering of a people who are on the lowest rung of the political and economic ladder and who survive by subsistence farming and selling souvenirs to tourists.

But the tide is turning. These disenfranchised and peaceful people are beginning to rediscover their own roots, weaving traditional Aztec designs into their folk patterns and restoring dimly remembered oral traditions of folklore and ritual.

And you can help them. As the Paris couturiers plunder Aztec designs for their catwalk collections, you can visit your local ethnic clothing store to buy the real, hand-crafted item, thereby feeding a handful of *centavos* back to the village communes that are being established to help put right centuries of wrong.

A
Spiritual
Civilization

———————— • ————————

AZTEC PHILOSOPHY sounds very familiar to Western ears: an ambassador from the Milky Way was sent by God with a message to the virgin Sochiquetzal to tell her that she would conceive and give birth to Quetzalcoatl, the Son of Heaven.

His true parent was God, the Universal Creator — whom the Aztecs considered both male and female. After his birth Quetzalcoatl was known as the Lord of the Winds, and he became the Aztecs' greatest priest-philospher-king. One of his his first acts was to summon two wise women, Cipactonal and Oxomoco, the revered cave-dwellers of Cuernavaca. Quetzalcoatl invited them to work with him to create calendars and day symbols so that his people could learn to read and write.

Cipactonal was given the immense honour of first choice. She painted Cipactli, the Alligator, while her friend Oxomoco chose Ecatl, the Wind. Their 20 'day pictures' became known as: Alligator, Wind, House, Lizard, Serpent, Death, Deer, Rabbit, Water, Dog, Monkey, Grass, Reed, Ocelot, Eagle, Vulture, Earthquake, Knife, Rain and Flower. And it was these day signs that became the basis of the strong tradition of astrology that the ancient Aztecs developed and explored to a precision unmatched today.

STAR-GAZERS

Aztecs considered astrology an essential part of their daily lives. From the moment that a baby was born, when its parents hastily summoned the *advino* (astrologer) to discern the child's fate and future, to the careful noting of daily predictions from annual almanacs, every child and adult accepted star-gazing as a routine feature of their life-styles.

The great Aztec kings were not only astrologers themselves: they established special psychic universities where students trained to interpret not only the movements of the stars in their heavens, but the true importance of omens like sacred numbers, storms, eclipses, comets and animal behaviour. Special ziggurats were built to study the movements of the heavenly bodies. After centuries of meticulous observation, the Aztecs calculated their solar year as lasting 365.2420 days, which is only 17.28 seconds short of absolute accuracy – an astonishing achievement for people lacking any form of scientific instrumentation to help them.

Away from the court, the vital role of astrologer in society was held by wise women, who were community leaders and magistrates with the king's authority to decide business matters and to act as mediators in divorce. Some of this tradition continues today in the 'Mex-Tex' system of astrology among ethnic Central American communities in the USA. Known as *Brujería* (Discoverers of Hidden Truths), it employs women known as *Brujas* (Witches or Wise Women), whose spotless moral reputations are seen as an essential part of their training and calling.

Two Aztec astrologers who were considered to be the equals of Quetzalcoatl were King Nazahualpilli of Tezcuco and King Montezuma. Ironically, we are given this fascinating insight by the infamous Spanish Grand Inquisitor Tomas de

Torquemada. (Confessor to Ferdinand ll and lsabella, Torquemada was notorious for his cruelty, bigotry, intolerance and religious fanaticism. A convert to Catholicism, Torquemada masterminded the expulsion of 160,000 fellow Jews and the torture of thousands.) ln his work, *Indian Monarch*, Torquemada records that King Nazahualpilli was

> a great astrologer and prided himself much on his knowledge of the motions of celestial bodies, and being attached to this study, that he caused enquiries to be made throughout the entire of his dominions, for all such persons as were at all conversant with it, whom he had brought to his court, and imparted to them whatever he knew, and ascending by night on the terraced roof of his palace, he thence considered the stars, and disputed with them on all difficult questions concerned with them.
>
> l at least can affirm that l have seen a place outside of the roof of the palace, enclosed within four walls only a yard in height and just of sufficient breadth for a man to lie down in; in each angle was a hole of perforation . . . and on inquiring the use of the square place, a grandson of his, who was showing me the palace, replied that it was for King Nazahualpilli, when he went by night, attended by his astrologers, to contemplate the heavens and the stars; whence l inferred that what was reported of him was true.

When Montezuma took up his crown it was his fellow King Nazahualpilli who congratulated this nation on the wisdom of their choice: 'a man whose deep knowledge of heavenly things insured to his subjects his comprehension of those of an earthly nature'.

Later it was this same fellow astrologer who warned Montezuma of the impending catastrophe. He prophesied that time was running out for the Aztec empire, and with the destruction of Montezuma's cities and the slaughter of his people, the old civilization of the country would disappear. Nazahualpilli added that bad omens and phenomena would appear in the coming years to confirm this dire prediction.

And so they did. Starting in AD 1505 (Julian calendar), there was a severe famine. When the new cycle began some two years later, an eclipse was seen – an omen of disaster for the Aztecs. This was followed by an earthquake and, in each succeeding year immediately prior to the Spanish invasion, a full quota of bad omens made themselves felt. The earthquake was followed by a comet, which 'with three heads travelled East'. Then a 'pyramid light which scattered sparks from all sides' rose on the Eastern horizon and stayed there for periods of over 40 days at a time. This was, according to the wise Aztec seers, a presage of 'wars, famine, pestilence, mortality among lords'.

Montezuma called on his fellow astrologer and once again King Nazahualpilli studied the heavens only to announce that he confirmed these findings. Neither Montezuma nor his kingdom would survive the coming cataclysm, he declared. Sadly, he was right. The last of these 'evil omens' appeared in 1519, the year of the Spanish Invasion. For several days a comet hung over what is now Mexico City. The threatened ruin, said the seers, was now inevitable.

For at least four generations before the Spanish arrived on these shores, prophecies were known that one day the country would be invaded by bearded men from across the sea, who would wear strange garments and 'caskets upon their heads'. These invaders would be heavily armed with sharp swords and would overrun the country and destroy the Aztec gods. Montezuma himself knew by prescience that cataclysm would end his rule. Revered by his people as a genius, he was a great general and statesman who had conquered 44 cities and welded them together into one great nation.

So when, in 1508, Montezuma was brought an ashen-faced, crane-like bird at his celestial school at Tlillancalmecatl ('a place of heavenly learning'), he knew it meant the beginning of the end. Scrying in the mirror-shaped crest on the bird's head, Montezuma at first saw reflected the heavens and the stars, and the fire sticks used to generate flame – an evil omen. Then the picture changed to show a concourse of warriors advancing, massed, as conquerors, in battle array. They were riding what – no Aztec having seen a horse – he described as a deer.

At about the same time Montezuma's sister, Paranzin, fell into a cataleptic trance. But as her funeral procession wound its way to the tomb, she suddenly recovered. While in trance, Paranzin had a vision in which she had seen great ships from a far country bring towards them men in foreign dress, armed and wearing metal casques on their heads and with banners in their hands.

So it was that when the Spanish finally arrived – in 1520 – the Aztecs knew what to expect, and that these invaders would become their masters. Soaked in generations of prophetic divination and despite the obvious fact that they vastly outnumbered the conquistadores, they offered the astonished Spanish little or no opposition. The great Montezuma – 'by nature wise, an astrologer and philosopher, and skilled and generally versed in all the arts, both in those military and those of a civil nature', died just as he had foreseen – toasted over a spit!

TIMEKEEPING

People who study the Mayan civilization are sometimes
confused by the fact that these ancient peoples had not one
but two calendars. The first was a solar calendar (see
overleaf) which dealt with agriculture, laws and finance. It
contained 18 months of precisely 20 days each, plus a further
five 'nameless' days (*Nemontemi*) at the end of this year,
making a familiar total of 365 days. This calendar was in use
35 years before the birth of Christ.

The Aztecs dealt with leap years by ignoring them — until
52 years had passed. Then they made up for the loss by
adding a further 13 days and celebrating. This was a special
festival, called Tying the Bundle, when a bunch of reeds was
tied together to mark the end of the 52 years, and all old fires
were extinguished and new ones lit.

THE SACRED CALENDAR

This system covered religious events, festivals and prediction.
It lasted 13 weeks, each containing a repeating cycle of 20
days named after the pictures drawn by the wise cave-
dwellers of Cuernavaca. This book is based upon the sacred
calendar still used today by the Quiche Mayans of Guatemala.

Converting Aztec dates to the Western Julian calendar is
complicated, since the two systems deal with the problem of
leap years in different ways. It's made even more complex by
different researchers offering conflicting systems of

calculations. Most students now accept the GMT (Goodman-Martinez-Thompson) method, which is the one l have used for calculations of celebrity birth data.

● THE SOLAR YEAR CALENDAR

Month	Name	Dates	Western equivalent*
1	Toxcatl	21 Apr–10 May	Taurus
2	Etzalqualiztli	11–30 May	Taurus + Gemini
3	Tecuhilhuitontli	31 May–19 June	Gemini
4	Hueitecuhilhuitl	20 June–9 July	Gemini + Cancer
5	Tlaxochimaco	10–29 July	Cancer + Leo
6	Xocotlhuetzi	30 July–18 Aug	Leo
7	Ochpaniztli	19 Aug–7 Sept	Leo + Virgo
8	Teotleco	8–27 Sept	Virgo + Libra
9	Tepeilhuitl	28 Sept–17 Oct	Libra
10	Quecholli	18 Oct–6 Nov	Libra + Scorpio
11	Panquetzaliztli	7–26 Nov	Scorpio + Sagittarius
12	Atemoztli	27 Nov–16 Dec	Sagittarius
13	Tititl	17 Dec–5 Jan	Sagittarius + Capricorn
14	Izcalli	6–25 Jan	Capricorn + Aquarius
15	Atlcoualco	26 Jan–14 Feb	Aquarius
16	Tlacaxipeualiztli	15 Feb–6 Mar	Aquarius + Pisces
17	Tozoztontli	7–26 Mar	Pisces + Aries
18	Huei Tozoztli	27 Mar–15 Apr	Aries
	Nemontemi	16–20 April	Aries

The Western zodiac equivalents given here are for information only. The Aztecs did not use this system for star-gazing. This was covered by the sacred calendar.

HOW TO DISCOVER YOUR AZTEC BIRTH SIGN

There are four ways to find out which of the 20 Aztec day signs relates to your birthday.

For fun and entertainment
Read the virtues and vices of each sign, then the lists of celebrities that follow, and try to decide which comes closest to you or those you care for.

For the curious who want to know more
Details of individual computer Aztec astrology print-outs are available from: Home Keys Publishing, P.O. Box 1407, Devizes, Wiltshire SN10 1ZA, UK.

For the serious star-gazer
If you have some experience of calculating Western zodiac systems, then you may want to attempt the complex calculations offered by K.C. Tunnicliffe in his *Aztec Astrology* (see the Bibliography).

For the computer user
The simplest way is to get all the calculations done for you by a computer program. There are two special programs available. One is a 'shareware' (try before you buy) disk available from: R.K. West, P.O. Box 8044, Mission Hills, CA 91346, USA. A more detailed program is available from: Astrolabe, Inc., P.O. Box 1750, 350 Underpass Road, Brewster, MA 02631, USA.

SIGN CHART

N

*Mental &
Analytical*

WIND
DEATH
DOG
KNIFE
OCELOT

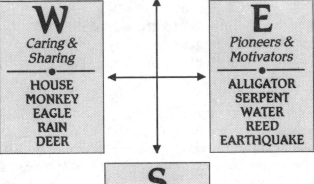

W

*Caring &
Sharing*

HOUSE
MONKEY
EAGLE
RAIN
DEER

E

*Pioneers &
Motivators*

ALLIGATOR
SERPENT
WATER
REED
EARTHQUAKE

S

*Sensitive &
Empathic*

LIZARD
RABBIT
GRASS
VULTURE
FLOWER

THE SIGNS

CIPACTLI
•
Alligator

**Pioneers and motivators
an Aztec day sign of the East**

CHARACTERISTICS

VIRTUES	VICES
Ambitious	Calculating
Dependable	Depressive
Determined	Greedy
Generous	Inhibited
Loyal	Materialistic
Patient	Mercenary
Practical	Neglectful
Self-controlled	Pessimistic
Self-reliant	Social-climbing
Stable	Unsympathetic
Trustworthy	

PERSONALITY

IF YOU ARE BORN UNDER this sign you can (like the alligator) be fiercely territorial, protecting both your rights and boundaries with great determination. No one should argue with the sons and daughters of Cipactli, unless they are prepared for a fight to the death!

The children of Alligator parents are well cared for, especially by their mothers, who guard their offspring with a determined eye. This can bring problems in later life when some of these 'warrior mothers' experience difficulty in letting go of their parental duties.

Alligator fathers like nothing more than to found dynasties, especially ones that will flourish long after their founder has passed on. Modern-day Alligators include Walt

Disney and Frank Sinatra. Some, however, can lose sight of reality in all this thrust for ambition, as happened to Nazi leader Albert Speer, eccentric financier Howard Hughes and the Yugoslavian dictator, Marshal Tito.

Interestingly, the Indian Hindu system of astrology has a similar sign. Named Makara (crocodile), it approximates to the traditional qualities of the more familiar Western sign of Capricorn. Both Aztec and Hindu systems agree that this sign governs rivers, forests, lakes, jungles and marshlands.

On the positive side, the Aztecs saw Alligator folk as generous, charitable, creative, constructive and very, very fertile. It's one of the highly sexed signs, with both sexes capable of great stamina and reproductive ability!

This is one of the most industrious signs in the Aztec world. Cipactli-born were famed for their application, determination and perspiration. It can be a restless kind of energy, which is constantly seeking a suitable home. Correctly harnessed in positive and productive outlets, here is the man or woman who happily abandons outworn habits to seek new ground. Just as the alligator of the Florida swamps thinks nothing of travelling 30 miles (48 km) to make a hole in which to trap fish during the dry season, those born under this day sign are famed for having the courage to open new doors.

The Aztecs believed that Alligators are loyal and faithful to their partners, as long as they feel emotionally secure. Deprive them of that, however, and your Alligator could rapidly become a couch potato.

Much hangs on the upbringing of those born under this sign. If their parents were overly critical, some Alligators may well want to explore therapy to release this resentment. Others develop a thick skin that can protect them from all but the most penetrating barbs. And those who dare to face them in contests should beware the 'gator's favourite trick of rotating their victims in water (or emotion) to drown them!

FAMOUS ALLIGATORS

MUSICIANS
Herb Alpert
Joan Baez
Johnny Cash
Aretha Franklin
Marvin Hamlisch
Simon Le Bon
Dame Nellie Melba
Nikolai Rimsky-Korsakov
Frank Sinatra

INVENTORS
Alexander Graham Bell
Christian Doppler
Thomas Alva Edison
Ferdinand von Zeppelin

ACTORS
John Cleese
Joan Crawford
Tom Hanks
Demi Moore
Sean Penn
Orson Welles

MOVIE-MAKERS
Walt Disney
Leni Riefenstahl
Jacques Tati

and . . .
Leonid Brezhnev
(Russian leader)
Samuel Taylor Coleridge
(poet)
Frederic Goudy
(type founder)
Howard Hughes
(tycoon and film-maker)
Douglas Hurd
(British politician)
Linus Pauling *(chemist)*
Olga Korbut *(gymnast)*
Rocky Marciano *(boxer)*
A.A. Milne
(children's author)

Friedrich Perls
(Gestalt analyst)
Henry Raymond
(New York Times editor)
John Ruskin *(writer and
social reformer)*
Boris Spassky
(chess grand master)
Sir George Stephen
(railway banker)

Sidney Gilchrist Thomas
(metallurgist)
Marshal Tito
(Yugoslavian leader)

and . . .
Nazis: Joachim von
Ribbentrop, Ernst Roehm
and Albert Speer

EHECATL
·
Wind

**Mental and analytical
an Aztec day sign of the North**

CHARACTERISTICS

VIRTUES	VICES
Charming	Critical
Conversational	Distracted
Flexible	Fanciful
Imaginative	Flirtatious
Intellectual	Gossipy
Inventive	Impetuous
Linguistic	Inconsiderate
Persuasive	Restless
Quick-witted	Superficial
Vivacious	Unreliable
Youthful	

PERSONALITY

THE SIMPLEST WAY to spot a Wind sign is to think words, dance, lyrics or music. If these form a major part of a person's life, especially if it is their job or vocation, then you're talking Ehecatl.

This is the sign of the communicator, someone with a hyperactive mind who can talk themselves right out of their cradle straight into the public eye (or ear). Wind folk are versatile, so much so that one of their main headaches is choosing which of their many talents to pursue. Often these sons and daughters of Ehecatl are so multi-gifted that settling for just one career on which to focus can be a major problem. This is where you find the college student with straight As in all their academic work, a leading slot in the sports team, plus an honours in music.

Highly intelligent and super-restless — just like the nature of the sign itself — all Wind-born can prove unpredictable at times. Here is unsettled energy, here is the need for much mental stimulation, and here you will find the mortal seeking his or her chance to conquer the elements.

The world's top writers, preachers, dancers, aviators, politicians, actors and singers all feel at home under the restless storm that is the Aztec Wind sign. Whatever their chosen skill, those who do make it to stardom have learned instinctively just how to harness this powerful natural element we call air, and they can offer us a symphony of soothing sound or a whirlwind storm, according to their whim. Some say that here are the real magicians of the twentieth century, elemental alchemists who can turn air into gold.

Just as the zodiac of the Western world offers us positive and negative examples of the 12 star signs, so too does the astrology of the Aztecs. And the negative side of the Wind-born can terrify, especially if the person has an obsession. Dictator Joseph Stalin terrorized Russia, while the Nazi propagandists Rudolf Hess and British broadcasting traitor William Joyce (Lord Haw Haw) were all Wind-born. The good news is that folk like these who sow their Wind do seem to reap it — eventually!

Relationships is one area where many Wind-born do seem to encounter difficulties. On the one hand is their urgent need for a stable partner to help balance all this untapped genius; while on the other is the mental taunting that they sometimes throw at their mates, just as a cat will use furniture as a scratching post — simply because it's there. It does need a strong partner to ignore this disruptive teasing.

One way to try to capture the essence of Aztec Wind is to picture the amazing footwork of Fred Astaire, add in the trumpet of Louis Armstrong, the reassuring voice of Nat King Cole, the sheer style of movie moguls Sam Goldwyn and Cecil B. de Mille, the legend of Casey Jones and the penmanship of that theatrical master, Noël Coward.

Two such men who battled with their element were the pioneering aviator Charles Lindbergh and British solo round-the-world yachtsman Sir Francis Chichester, both of whom harnessed wind to achieve personal satisfaction.

Wind women are equally amazing, as shown by the golden tonsils of Josephine Baker, Roberta Flack, Kylie Minogue, Joan Armatrading, Tammy Wynette and Neneh Cherry; the pioneering suffragette Emmeline Pankhurst; controversial feminist writer Erica Jong (who, as a Wind child, can't really 'fear' flying); the talented sculptress Dame Barbara Hepworth; and the actresses Lauren Bacall and Elizabeth Taylor.

FAMOUS WIND CHILDREN

ACTORS
Lauren Bacall
Matthew Broderick
Richard Burton
Sir Noël Coward
Sir John Gielgud
Sir Alec Guinness
Elizabeth Taylor
Sir Herbert Beerbohm Tree

SINGERS
Joan Armatrading
Josephine Baker
Neneh Cherry
Judy Collins
Sam Cooke
Bryan Ferry
Roberta Flack
Michael Jackson
Kylie Minogue
Nina Simone
Gene Vincent
Slim Whitman
Tammy Wynette

MOVIE MOGULS
Cecil B. de Mille
Sam Goldwyn
George Lucas

WRITERS
R.F. Delderfield
Erica Jong
T.E. Lawrence
Ross Macdonald
Ezra Pound
J.B. Priestley
Harold Robbins
Algernon Charles Swinburne
Gay Talese
John Updike
Noah Webster
Herman Wouk

MUSICIANS
Louis Armstrong
Dave Brubeck
Eric Clapton
Nat King Cole
Mantovani
Paul McCartney
Johann Strauss Jr
Lawrence Welk
Frank Zappa

PIONEERS
Sir Francis Chichester
Charles Lindbergh
Emmeline Pankhurst

ENTREPRENEURS
Richard Jordan Gatling
William Randolph Hearst
Casey Jones
Valdemar Poulsen
Julius Rosenwald
Ernst Friedrich Schumacher
Elmer Ambrose Sperry
Ellsworth Milton Statler

WHIRLWINDS
Lord Haw Haw
(Nazi propagandist)
Rudolf Hess *(Nazi leader)*
Joseph Stalin
(Russian dictator)
Walter Ulbricht
(East German politician)

POLITICIANS
Harry S. Truman
Sir Robert Walpole

and . . .
Fred Astaire *(dancer)*
Anne Frank
(Jewish diarist)
Billy Graham *(evangelist)*
Dame Barbara Hepworth
(sculptress)
Thurgood Marshall
(judge)
Arnold Palmer
(golfer)
Charles M. Schulz
(cartoonist)

CALLI
•
House

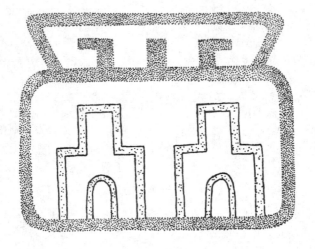

**Caring and sharing
an Aztec day sign of the West**

CHARACTERISTICS

VIRTUES	VICES
Fertile	Cloying
Intuitive	Hypochondriac
Loving	Lazy
Loyal	Moody
Maternal	Self-centred
Nourishing	Self-pitying
Patient	Selfish
Protective	Shrewd
Sensitive	Slavish
Sympathetic	Timid
Tender	
Thrifty	

PERSONALITY

SECURITY IS THE KEY to a happy House person. This one factor above all others is the one they crave and need in order to flourish. It means a base where they can settle and plan. With this vital issue resolved, the House-born are both peaceful and peace loving. Not for them the creative tensions of their more artistic brothers and sisters; not for them the agonies of the struggling author locked in a draughty attic. The perfect House mother and House father want no more than a successful mate and a goodly clutch of chicks to nurture and cherish.

But don't for a second think of them as boring, for this is the Aztec sign that contains distinguished names like

Abraham Lincoln, Queen Elizabeth I, British Prime Minister William Gladstone, the South African politician and Nobel Peace Prize winner F.W. de Klerk and Eva Perón — House-born who took their need to nurture to nations.

There's a distinct physical presence about House folk. Some have sheer animal magnetism and sexual charisma; some may dress to kill; while others patiently strive to become teachers, pioneers and leaders.

House folk are house proud: that's a fact of life and just as true in the twentieth century as it was hundreds of years ago in Mayan civilizations. They will fuss and cluck over their homes and partners and children; even if it can at times seem like whines and moans, it is simply their way of expressing the caring that comes from having a big heart.

House folk *care*. And it all starts from a having a secure home life. Once this vital need is established — and patience is just one of the many House virtues — then many of these people will start planning which corner of the globe they are going to adopt and spread their nurture.

That great Anglo-American institution, the broadcaster Alistair Cooke, has used his ability to nurture an understanding between two nations divided by a common language. Then there's the Wind daughter Jennifer Rush, whose songs tell us about the nurturing power of love.

Like politicians, House-born musicians offer nurture to nations: Richard Wagner is Germany to many people, just as Sergei Prokofiev is Russia; while Art Garfunkel sings nostalgically for America and gives us timeless and unmistakable tunes.

Australian dancer Robert Helpmann nurtured ballet and won a knighthood. English champion jockey Gordon Richards won his knighthood for the nurture he invested in his sport; Brazilian football owes just as much to its Wind-born maestro Pelé. America owes a debt to the caring skills of architect Frank Lloyd Wright.

FAMOUS HOUSE DWELLERS

MUSICIANS
Don Everly
Art Garfunkel
Coleman Hawkins
Quincy Jones
George Michael
Jacques Offenbach
Charlie Parker
Sergei Prokofiev
Jennifer Rush
Buffy Sainte-Marie
Rod Stewart
Georg Philipp Telemann
Richard Wagner
Boxcar Willie
Bill Wyman

ACTORS
Olivia de Havilland
Marlene Dietrich
Michael Caine
Marius Goring
Gina Lollobrigida
Telly Savalas
Sarah Siddons

BROADCASTERS
Alistair Cooke
Jane Pauley
Dan Rather

WRITERS
Eric Ambler
Robert Browning
Erskine Caldwell
Henry James
Jerome K. Jerome
Jack Kerouac
Charles Lamb
Ursula Le Guin
Thomas Mann
Alan Paton
Arthur Schopenhauer
Neil Simon
Muriel Spark
Sir Stephen Spender
H.G. Wells
Walt Whitman
John Wyndham

MOVIE-MAKERS
John Ford
Sir David Lean
Adolph Zukor

ARTISTS
Leonardo da Vinci
Stanley William Hayter
Edouard Manet
Michelangelo
Jean-François Millet

GOVERNMENT
Fidel Castro
Catherine the Great
Queen Elizabeth 1
William Ewart Gladstone
F.W. de Klerk
Abraham Lincoln
Eva Perón

INVENTORS
Edward Jenner
Robert Koch
Friedrich Krupp
Samuel Morse
Charles Pathé
Sir William Perkin

and . . .
Marie Antoinette *(consort)*
Yuri Gagarin *(astronaut)*
Robert Helpmann
(ballet dancer)
James Hoffa
(Teamster trade unionist)
Joe Louis *(boxer)*
Sir Edwin Lutyens *(architect)*
Pelé *(footballer)*
Wendell Phillips *(reformer)*
Joseph Banks Rhine
(parapsychologist)
Sir Gordon Richards
(jockey)
Julius Rosenberg (spy)
Frank Lloyd Wright
(architect)

CUETZPALLIN
·
Lizard

**Sensitive and empathic
an Aztec day sign of the South**

CHARACTERISTICS

VIRTUES	VICES
Analytical	Boastful
Brave	Fanatical
Courageous	Jealous
Creative	Obsessive
Dynamic	Revengeful
Magnetic	Ruthless
Principled	Secretive
Profound	Sexually demanding
Resourceful	Venomous
Sincere	
Strong-willed	

PERSONALITY

THIS IS one of the Aztec signs of passion. Here is the fervour of determination, fuelled by intensity. These are the folk who refuse to take No for an answer. Whatever they choose, they do it with everything they have; there are no short cuts for the Lizard: it just has to be all or nothing.

This all-consuming passion can be (and is) applied with equal application to both bedroom and boardroom. Whether it be the vituperative passion of self-exiled US writer Gore Vidal or the spiritual passion of civil rights leader Martin Luther King, the burning need to apply themselves to an issue is the hallmark of Cuetzpallin.

This is the Aztec sign of leadership. Babies born on Lizard days seem to leap from their cradles with a general's baton in

their tiny fists. These folk seldom know fear: that's for lesser mortals. They believe that nothing is impossible, and history would seem to prove them right.

Lizards set great store in personal performance. They will create targets that lesser mortals think impossible. Whether they choose to lead a nation or their community, we can rest assured that we are in excellent hands.

The Aztecs believed that Lizards instinctively understood human foibles, weaknesses and faults. This made them ideal candidates to counsel others without judgement. From this it was but a short step to community leadership, such was the trust that others confidently placed in them.

This same passion, if not positively harnessed, could backfire upon Lizards and turn them into sex-mad satyrs or nymphomaniacs. Aztec parents of Lizard children were advised to take great care to guide their children to productive ways of handling all this intensity. The same applies today. Even on a small scale, such intensity that has yet to find its home can be exhausting to partners worn out by the demands of this unsatisfied passion.

But if all this fertility *is* turned to positive use, then the Lizard transforms into the higher personality that becomes the super-achiever, ready to tackle all odds in the search for the ultimate truth. Chances are that all this passion will be applied in a finely focused approach. Cuetzpallin may take ages to choose the sector of life that he or she wants to explore and improve upon, but once that choice has been made, then nothing will stop the Lizard from turning this interest into a lifetime's dedication to the ultimate benefit of humanity.

These folk are seldom superficial. They have a burning need to get to the very crux of everything that captures their interest. How does it work and why? What makes him/her tick? Who governs us and why? These are the deep issues that drive a Lizard to find the answers.

FAMOUS LIZARDS

ARTISTS
Sir John Everett Millais
Pierre Auguste Renoir
Ronald Searle

WRITERS
Sir Arthur Conan Doyle
Eric von Däniken
F. Scott Fitzgerald
Horace Greeley
Vaclav Havel
E. Nesbit
Victoria Sackville-West
Gore Vidal

POETS
T.S. Eliot
George William Russell

MUSICIANS
Edvard Grieg
Oscar Hammerstein ll
Mstislav Rostropovich
Robert Schumann
Giuseppe Verdi

SINGERS
Chuck Berry
Beniamino Gigli
Otis Redding
Dame Joan Sutherland

ACTORS
Bill Cosby
Greta Garbo
Leonard Nimoy
Nancy Reagan

GOVERNMENT
Queen Elizabeth ll
John Maynard Keynes
Ramsay MacDonald
Dean Rusk
Jan Smuts

MOVIE-MAKERS
Fritz Lang
Jean Renoir

PIONEERS & ENTREPRENEURS

Christiaan Barnard
(heart surgeon)
Christian Dior *(couturier)*
Peter Fabergé *(jeweller)*
Harvey S. Firestone
(automotive engineer)
George Gallup *(pollster)*
Martin Luther King
(civil rights activist)
Dame Alicia Markova
(ballerina)

Andrew Mellon *(financier)*
Wilhelm Messerschmitt
(plane designer)
Ernst Werner von Siemens
(industrialist)
Arnold Toynbee
(historian)

and . . .
Johnny Carson
Joseph Goebbels
Cardinal Francis Spellman

COATL
·
Serpent

**Pioneers and motivators
an Aztec day sign of the East**

CHARACTERISTICS

VIRTUES	VICES
Charismatic	Devious
Courageous	Egomaniacal
Determined	Hypersensitive
Dynamic	Obsessive
Humanitarian	Over-sexed
Inventive	Power-tripping
Philanthropic	Revengeful
Principled	Ruthless
Resourceful	Secretive
Sensual	Self-destructive
Sexual	

PERSONALITY

THE AZTECS believed that the Serpent-born represented sex, fertility and beauty. There could be a link here between this interpretation and the Chinese system of astrology, which sees Serpent (or Snake) women as the most sexually charismatic of the 12 signs.

This day of Coatl is governed by the Goddess Chalchiuhtlicue, the water goddess with a jewelled robe. Her sons and daughters are fair of face and keep their astounding vigour well into later life.

Serpents are the innovators who see an opportunity and exploit it, then recycle their profits into humanitarian philanthropy.

There's great emotional power at the disposal of the Serpent. It can be used to mesmerize either partners or the public. Used wisely, it can benefit humankind; used negatively, it can both manipulate and dominate. Serpent people's main problem lies in their personal lives. These romantics can waste a lifetime chasing emotional illusions or repeat destructive partnership patterns and yet never seem to learn.

Crisis and confrontation seem to be the main preoccupations of Serpents. Just as their protective goddess was identified with sudden storms, so too do these folk encounter dramatic turning-points in their lives. The manner in which they handle these dramas is a learning curve for all to observe.

Sex is another focus for Coatl. Mae West, Madame du Barry and Marilyn Monroe were Serpents, as are the French romantic balladeer, Charles Aznavour and the pelvis-gyrating singer Tom Jones.

Strength is another factor that typifies the Serpent. Sylvester Stallone was Coatl-born and so were Clint Eastwood and naval hero Lord Nelson.

There's curiosity and inventiveness within this sign, as the following lists reveal.

FAMOUS SERPENTS

MUSICIANS
Frédéric Chopin
George Frideric Handel
Gustav Holst
Franz Liszt
André Previn

SINGERS
Charles Aznavour
Andy Gibb
Deborah Harry
Shirley Jones
Tom Jones
Luciano Pavarotti
Lionel Ritchie
Cat Stevens

ACTORS
Tom Cruise
Clint Eastwood
John Huston
Marilyn Monroe
Sylvester Stallone
Mae West

WRITERS
Leslie Charteris
Monica Dickens
Christopher Fry
Dame Ngaio Marsh
Arthur Miller

Aleksandr Pushkin
Dorothy L. Sayers
Upton Sinclair
Anthony Trollope
Horace Walpole
Jakob Wassermann

INNOVATORS
Sir Robert Baden-Powell
(Founder of Scouting)
Heinrich Hertz
(physicist)
James P. Joule
(physicist)
W.K. Kellogg
(food)
Sir Thomas Lipton
(grocer and philanthropist)
André Michelin *(tyres)*
Sir Flinders Petrie
(archaeologist)
Dame Marie Rambert
(ballerina)
Wilhelm Reich
(psychologist)
Margaret Sanger
(birth control pioneer)
Igor Sikorsky
(helicopter designer)
Adam Smith
(economist)

POLITICIANS
Sir Anthony Eden
Barry Goldwater
Ulysses S. Grant
(18th US President)
Norman Lamont
David Mellor
Shimon Peres
Sun Yat-sen
Charles Maurice de
Talleyrand-Périgord

and . . .
John Dee
*(Elizabethan astrologer and
spymaster)*
Comtesse du Barry
(mistress of Louis XV)
Jean Paul Getty
(millionaire art collector)
Horatio Nelson *(admiral)*
Pope Pius XI
Knud Rasmussen
(Danish arctic explorer)
Dutch Schultz *(gangster)*
Edward Wyllis Scripps
(publisher)
Arthur Sulzberger
(New York Times publisher)

MIQUIZTLI

Death

**Mental and analytical
an Aztec day sign of the North**

CHARACTERISTICS

VIRTUES	VICES
Caring	Dominating
Humble	Fearful
Leader	Indecisive
Patient	Indifferent
Responsible	Introverted
Sensitive	Over-cautious
Socially aware	Selfish
Stamina	Subversive
Strategic	Unlucky
Thoughtful	

PERSONALITY

FEW OF THE PEOPLE born under this sign are actually involved in death. The notable exceptions are the small-arms manufacturer Samuel Colt, Gulf War general (Sir) Colin Powell, the suicidal pop singer Sid Vicious and Margaret Fox (one of the sisters responsible for modern spiritualism). The rest of Miquiztli's sons and daughters are actually too busy being involved in rebirth!

The real message for those born under this particular Aztec sign is the Death of the *ego* and its transformation into helping others – as seen in the lives of men like Sir Robert Peel (creator of Britain's police force) and former UN Secretary-General U Thant.

The poems of Robert Frost explain more; the music of Richard Rodgers adds harmony; and the voice of Ella

Fitzgerald brings warmth — all three of whom were born under Miquiztli.

It's a sign that is often preoccupied with the deeper mysteries of life. These folk are seldom content to sit back and accept what is on offer. Instead, they are driven to probe and explore.

Admittedly, this outlook does tend to bring a more serious approach to life and its responsibilities, but the product of all this gravitas and pondering brings a true awareness of how communities work and how best they can be improved.

Shy and hesitant in early life, Miquiztlis are often late developers, but when they do blossom, it's not like the fleeting flourish of the hot-house flower. Here we find the solid citizens of today and tomorrow, those men and women who are determined to set out to change our world, almost as if they feel an unseen hand prompting them onwards, and any opposition soon fades because these are the people who have done their homework thoroughly.

Many of the sons and daughter of Miquiztli are night birds, content to plan, study and fill those moonlit evenings with their strategies for the morrow. Here are the list makers, the forward planners and the dreamers of dreams that one day will be fulfilled.

Miquiztlis are security conscious, especially in relationships where they may be initially reluctant to commit, yet remain loyal when many less well-founded relationships have faded away. Here are the therapists and counsellors who have already climbed that mountain we call awareness and who can offer us solid guidance from first-hand knowledge. These folk know, because they have been there. The rest of us would do well to listen to them.

FAMOUS DEATH PEOPLE

MUSICIANS
Sir Thomas Beecham
Ludwig van Beethoven
Irving Berlin
Jerome Kern
Richard Rodgers
John Philip Sousa

SINGERS
Jane Birkin
Belinda Carlisle
Jason Donovan
Marianne Faithful
José Feliciano
Ella Fitzgerald
Matt & Luke Goss
Cyndi Lauper
Trini Lopez
Freddie Mercury
Alison Moyet
Alan Price
P.J. Proby
Nancy Sinatra
Sid Vicious
Marty Wilde

ACTORS
Jane Fonda
Hayley Mills
Paul Robeson
Liv Ullman

WRITERS
J.P. Donleavy
Daphne du Maurier
Robert Frost
Johann Wolfgang von Goethe
John D. MacDonald
W. Somerset Maugham
John McPhee
Boris Pasternak
Frederic Pohl
Mordecai Richler
Evelyn Underhill
Sir Hugh Walpole
P.G. Wodehouse
Christa Wolf

PAINTERS & ILLUSTRATORS
Paul Gauguin
Holman Hunt
Maxfield Parrish
Arthur Rackham
Sir Joshua Reynolds

POLITICIANS
George Bush
Valéry Giscard d'Estaing
Gamal Abdel Nasser
Sir Robert Peel
U Thant
Kurt Waldheim

and . . .
Princess Anne
Samuel Colt *(gunsmith)*
Margaret Fox
(spiritualist)
Guglielmo Marconi
(physicist)
Sir Colin Powell
(Gulf War hero)
Eddie Rickenbacker *(aviator)*

John D. Rockefeller
*(industrialist and
philanthropist)*
Ethel Greenglass Rosenberg
(spy)
Clement Studebaker
(car manufacturer)
Paul Volcker *(economist)*
Sir Christopher Wren
(architect)

MAZATL

·

Deer

**Caring and sharing
an Aztec day sign of the West**

CHARACTERISTICS

VIRTUES	VICES
Caring	Cloying
Faithful	Demanding
Humanitarian	Depressive
Loving	Insecure
Loyal	Masochistic
Maternal	Over-sensitive
Nourishing	Retiring
Sincere	Selfish
Sympathetic	Slavish
Tender	Unambitious
Thrifty	

PERSONALITY

JUST LIKE its creature namesake, those born under this Aztec sign can be both timid and shy, especially in early life. Once this is overcome, then they search out ways of bringing benefits to their communities. Prince Charles is a classic example.

The negative side of Deer – where the person sets out to abuse rather than assist – can be seen in Wild West outlaw Jesse James, the agitator Malcom X and the 'bad guy' images portrayed by film star Edward G. Robinson. One Doe who misled her community was the evangelical Aimée Semple McPherson.

This concept of community caring often reflects itself in inventions to make life simpler for humankind. Examples of

Deer who have followed this path include the French photographic masters Daguerre and Lumière, the German automobile perfectionist Gottlieb Daimler, American food innovator Clarence Birdseye and the housewife's hero, washing-machine maker Frederick Maytag.

Their insular childhood enables Deers to look within for strength and then share their discoveries, especially in the creative arts. The classic work *Black Beauty* by Anna Sewell, the embracing poetry of Henry Wadsworth Longfellow, the unrepentant jingoism of statesman Harold Macmillan and the homeliness of English-born comedian Bob Hope, all reflect the external nurturing offered to us by the Mazatl-born.

There's tenderness here. There's also much gentleness, although normally this seems to be reserved for partners, who are an essential ingredient for any Deer to thrive. Some of these people often try several relationships before finding the perfect partner, and this can cost them dear!

Personal space is equally vital. Encroach on the Deer's chosen territory at your peril, for then you may well see an impressive warning and aggressive display of their formidable antlers.

FAMOUS DEER

MUSICIANS
Sir Eugene Goosens
Sergei Rachmaninov
Johann Strauss Sr

SINGERS
John Denver
David Essex
Elton John
Clodagh Rodgers
Sade
Dinah Shore
Dusty Springfield

COMEDIANS
Bob Hope
Eric Morecambe
Mel Smith

INNOVATORS
Clarence Birdseye *(food)*
Louis Daguerre
(photographer)
Gottlieb Daimler *(cars)*
Louis Lumière
(photographer)
Frederick Maytag
(washing-machines)
Sir William Siemens
(engineer)
Leland Stanford *(railways)*

WRITERS
Lewis Carroll
William Cobbett
Simone de Beauvoir
Allen Ginsberg
Henry Wadsworth
Longfellow
James A. Michener
V.S. Pritchett
Anna Sewell
Sir Philip Sidney
Alan Sillitoe
Stendhal
Richard Purdy Wilbur

POLITICIANS
Hugh Gaitskell
Helmut Kohl
Paul Kruger
Harold Macmillan
Enoch Powell
Pierre Trudeau

FINANCIERS &
INDUSTRIALISTS
Theodore Schultz
Charles Schwab
Edmund Clarence Stedman

and . . .
Prince Charles
John K. Galbraith
(economist and diplomat)
Lionel Hampton
(bandleader)
Jesse James *(outlaw)*
Niki Lauda *(racing driver)*
Aimée Semple McPherson
(evangelist)

Princess Margaret
Sir Stanley Matthews
(footballer)
Otto Preminger
(film director)
Galina Ulanova
(ballerina)
Malcolm X
(civil rights activist)

TOCHTLI
Rabbit

Sensitive and empathic
an Aztec day sign of the South

CHARACTERISTICS

VIRTUES	VICES
Artistic	Alcoholic
Caring	Drug abuser
Charming	Escapist
Clever	Gambler
Creative	Manipulative
Funny	Over-indulgent
Inventive	Over-sexed
Joyful	Risk taker
Romantic	
Saintly	
Sociable	

PERSONALITY

MOST OF these Aztec signs reflect aspects of the creature, element or object after which they are named. Rabbit, however, is an exception. This is *not* the sign of the timid (the ancient Mayans allocated that place to Deer); in fact the opposite, for here you will often find the gambler or, at the very least, the calculated risk taker — even in their careers.

There's determination and even vocational dedication here. This sign houses at least one saint, Mother Teresa, and several war-mongers, like the Prussian Grand Admiral Alfred von Tirpitz, as well as millionaires, like hotelier Conrad Hilton, and the philanthropist, Simon Guggenheim.

Tochtli is an excellent sign for singers and entertainers,

and many of its sons and daughters have achieved international recognition: Elvis Presley, Jimi Hendrix, Bette Midler, Whitney Houston, Joan Collins, Johnny Ray, Chubby Checker and Glen Campbell were all Rabbit-born.

There's a romantic flavour here, as seen in the poetry of Percy Bysshe Shelley and Sir Walter Scott, and in the plaintive love songs of Johnny Ray, Spanish singer Julio Iglesias and the French *'papillon'*, Edith Piaf.

On the negative side, Rabbits can indulge in self-destruction, often drink or drugs — Presley and Piaf again. Positive Rabbits can turn to humour to help us laugh at ourselves (which is said to be a sign of growing up), like humorist James Thurber, 'Nonsense' poet Edward Lear, contemporary TV comedians Paul Hogan and Pamela Stephenson in Australia, Harry Enfield in Britain and Steve Martin in America — not forgetting the late Buster Keaton.

The mind of a Rabbit is a complex and wonderful thing. It straddles the universe of human experience from humour to sorrow, and it can surprise even its owner. Politicians of international importance can be found here, like Eduard Shevardnadze and Alexei Kosygin. It contains inventors, like food-canner Henry John Heinz; couturiers, like Pierre Balmain; and suffragettes, like Sylvia Pankhurst.

FAMOUS RABBITS

WRITERS
Honoré de Balzac
John Dryden
E.M. Forster
Edward Lear
Norman Mailer
George Orwell
Beatrix Potter
Philip Roth
Carl Sandburg
Sir Walter Scott
Sidney Sheldon
Percy Bysshe Shelley
Virginia Woolf

INNOVATORS & ENTREPRENEURS
Pierre Balmain *(couturier)*
John Baskerville
(typographer)
Simon Guggenheim
(philanthropist)
Henry Heinz
(canned food)
Conrad Hilton
(hotelier)
Adolf Ochs
(newspaper publisher)
Carl Sagan *(scientist)*
David Sarnoff
(broadcasting)

SINGERS
Glen Campbell
Chubby Checker
Jimi Hendrix
Whitney Houston
Julio Iglesias
Edith Piaf
Elvis Presley
Johnny Ray
Don Williams

HUMORISTS
Harry Enfield
Paul Hogan
Buster Keaton
Steve Martin
Bette Midler
Pamela Stephenson
James Thurber

and . . .
Joan Collins
(actress)
David Garrick
(theatre)
William Hogarth
(engraver)
Billie Jean King
(tennis champion)
Alexei Kosygin
(politician)
Le Corbusier
(architect)
Robert E. Lee
(general)

Sylvia Pankhurst
(suffragette)
Max Reinhardt
(theatre)
Nelson Rockefeller
(politician)
Eduard Shevardnadze
(politician)
Mother Teresa
(saint)
Alfred von Tirpitz
(admiral)
Maurice Utrillo
(artist)

ATL
•
Water

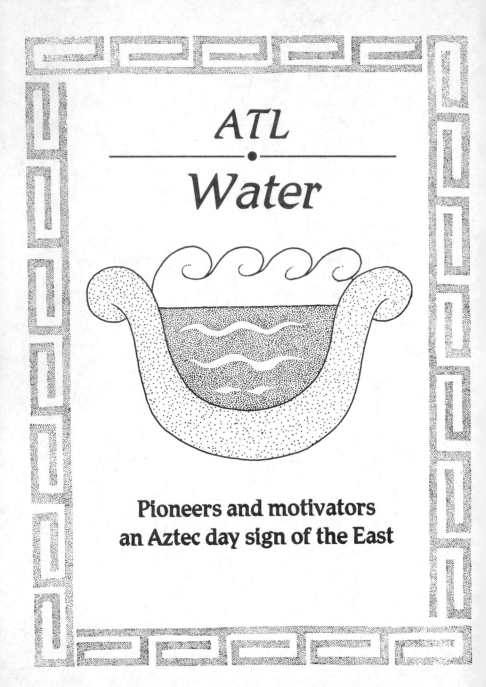

**Pioneers and motivators
an Aztec day sign of the East**

CHARACTERISTICS

VIRTUES	VICES
Caring	Dominating
Dedicated	Drama queen
Empathic	Exhibitionist
Generous	Introverted
Humanitarian	Manipulative
Innovative	Obsessive
Interpretive	Self-centred
Methodical	Short-tempered
Psychic	Unpredictable
Sensitive	Unpunctual
Worldly wise	Unreliable
	Unworthy

PERSONALITY

MEAN, MAGNIFICENT AND MOODY: that's the popular interpretation of those born under the Aztec sign of Atl. There's showmanship and charismatic style in the knapsacks of these Water babies and it all has to come out – one day. You cannot contain Water; it has to flow. These folk must have some outlet for their dreams and ambitions, or else they could well implode.

To get some feel for this almost theatrical hunger for an audience, just examine some of the diverse personalities who have felt this Water-born urge to express themselves dynamically: artist Salvador Dali, dancer Isadora Duncan,

actor Al Jolson, singers Mick Jagger and Madonna, dancer John Travolta, ballerina Anna Pavlova, comedian Mack Sennett and movie mogul D.W. Griffith were all born under this, at times, dramatic sign.

Atl explores the extremes in the human condition; two of its sons were the gangster Al Capone and the detective Allan Pinkerton. Here too you will find authors driven to write imaginatively: Margaret Mitchell *(Gone with the Wind)* and P.L. Travers *(Mary Poppins)*.

Whether it be in dreams or in the lakes, rivers, canals and oceans that surround us, Water has long been seen as a symbol for emotion, and who better to interpret this for us than the sons and daughters of Atl; singers with characteristic grand style and that elusive ability to touch the public's heartstrings and who entertain us with theatrical panache: like John Lennon, Liza Minnelli, Rick Springfield, Johnny Otis, Eartha Kitt and Sarah Vaughan.

Water contains politicians who can also command a sense of the theatrical; Presidents George Washington, Jefferson Davis and Bill Clinton wave the American flag, while the raffish former British Prime Minister Benjamin Disraeli and French Eurochef Jacques Delors reflect the old world.

Atl people are the self-inspired goal achievers, the dreamers of dreams who know that the secret of success lies not in the transformation of base metals into gold but in the modern alchemy of hard work and determination.

The Water-born have the gift of tuning into the human subconscious and producing genius from its flow. Just as this natural element can be harnessed with canals or hydro-electric power, these folk can tap the psyche to produce great works.

It's an all-or-nothing sign, with independence as one of its main cornerstones.

FAMOUS WATER BABIES

WRITERS
Elizabeth Barrett Browning
Joseph Conrad
Gustave Flaubert
John Keats
Margaret Mitchell
Christina Rossetti
William Makepeace
Thackeray
P.L. Travers
Izaak Walton
Henry Watterson
Arnold Wesker
Frank Yerby

ARTISTS
Salvador Dali
Sir Edwin Landseer

POLITICIANS
Jacques Delors
Benjamin Disraeli
Michael Foot
Rajiv Gandhi
Ian Paisley

US PRESIDENTS
Bill Clinton
Jefferson Davis
George Washington

INNOVATORS & ENTREPRENEURS
Louis Braille
(alphabet for visually handicapped)
Sir John Cockcroft
(hovercraft)
Sir Humphry Davy
(mining lamp)
Isadora Duncan *(dancer)*
George Eastman
(photographer)
D.W. Griffith *(movie-maker)*
Henry Irving
(actor-manager)
Joseph Lister *(surgeon)*
Allan Pinkerton *(detective)*
Mack Sennett *(movie-maker)*
Thomas Telford
(civil engineer)
Cornelius Vanderbilt
(transport magnate)

ACTORS
Jean Paul Belmondo
Gary Cooper
Rock Hudson
George C. Scott
Brooke Shields
Max Von Sydow
John Travolta

SINGERS	and . . .
Ian Drury	Al Capone *(gangster)*
Burl Ives	Thor Heyerdahl *(explorer)*
Mick Jagger	Stirling Moss *(racing driver)*
Al Jolson	Rupert Murdoch
Grace Jones	*(media mogul)*
Eartha Kitt	Anna Pavlova *(ballerina)*
John Lennon	Erwin Rommel
Madonna	*(Nazi general)*
Liza Minnelli	Bertrand Russell
Johnny Otis	*(philosopher)*
Kenny Rogers	H. Norman Schwarzkopf
Carly Simon	*(Gulf War commander)*
Rick Springfield	Alfred Stieglitz
Sarah Vaughan	*(photographer)*
Neil Young	

ITZCUINTLI

·

Dog

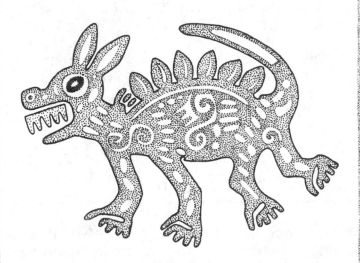

Mental and analytical
an Aztec day sign of the North

CHARACTERISTICS

VIRTUES	VICES
Artistic	Aggressive
Compassionate	Determined
Concerned	Dogmatic
Creative	Dominating
Faithful	Insensitive
Humanitarian	Manipulative
Leader	Parochial
Loyal	Scheming
Philosophical	Tenacious
Political	Threatening
Protective	
Supportive	

PERSONALITY

THE DOG-BORN are blessed. The ancients believed that these loyal companions would accompany their friends on their journey into the next world. This is the Aztec repository for the generous, the prosperous and the humanitarian.

Just like the domestic pet, Dogs like to have clearly identified territories, their own patch, which they will defend aggressively. The Dog role of honour clearly reflects what happens when those born under this Aztec sign choose their territories negatively or positively.

Starting with the infamous Dogs, Italian schemer Niccolò Machiavelli belongs here; so does his French counterpart Cardinal Jules Mazarin. But the most despised were the Nazi field marshal Hermann Goering and his master Adolf Hitler. These were Aztec canines with territorial hungers that eventually backfired.

The balancing factor lies with those good Dogs who fought for their countries' rights to freedom and self-government, like India's Mahatma Gandhi, Israel's Golda Meir and the Polish statesman Jan Paderewski.

The female of the species can be equally determined. Nursing heroine Florence Nightingale tops this list. She is joined by the English social reformer Elizabeth Fry, American educationalist Elizabeth Peabody and Australian feminist Germaine Greer.

Many of the Dog-born have important relationships with their fathers. These can be tumultuous or supportive — either way, this is one puppy whose outlook on life is heavily influenced by his or her Pa.

Not only do Itzcuintli offer faithfulness, they have the knack of generating it among their friends and workers. Many chief executives have envied the worker loyalty generated by top Dogs.

This canine-type stamina is one ingredient of creativity, and a number of Dogs have left their literary paw prints, from the gentle Kate Greenaway (children's book illustrator) to poets like John Milton and the Welsh Dylan Thomas and heavyweights of the calibre of Mark Twain, Henry Miller, G.K. Chesterton, Damon Runyon and Jonathan Swift.

TOP DOGS

SINGERS
Sammy Davis Jr
Bob Marley
Willie Nelson
Mike Oldfield
Leo Sayer
Toni Tenille

MUSICIANS
Georges Bizet
Sir Andrew Lloyd Webber
Ignace Jan Paderewski
Sir Malcolm Sargent
Pyotr Tchaikovsky
Vangelis

ACTORS
Richard Chamberlain
Maurice Chevalier
Harrison Ford
Richard Widmark

COUTURIERS
Elsa Schiaparelli
Charles Frederick Worth

LEADERS
Mahatma Gandhi
Golda Meir
William Pitt the Elder

WRITERS
Edgar Rice Burroughs
G.K. Chesterton
John Galsworthy
Germaine Greer
Alex Hayley
Henry Miller
John Milton
Damon Runyon
Jonathan Swift
Dylan Thomas
Mark Twain

PAINTERS & ILLUSTRATORS
John Constable
Jean Baptiste Corot
Kate Greenaway
James Tissot

PHILOSOPHERS & PHILANTHROPISTS
Friedrich Engels
Friedrich Froebel
Elizabeth Fry
Florence Nightingale
Elizabeth Peabody

MEDIA
Richard Dimbleby
Lord Northcliffe

INNOVATORS
Joseph Grimaldi *(clown)*
Sir Fred Hoyle *(astronomer)*
Joseph Marie Jacquard
(loom designer)
Willard Libby *(chemist)*
Friedrich Anton Mesmer
(hypnotist)
Isaac Meritt Singer
(sewing-machine designer)
Marie Tussaud *(waxworks)*
Wilbur Wright *(aviator)*

FINANCE
Sir Samuel Cunard
(shipping magnate)
Jacques Necker
(banker)
Lewis Thompson Preston
(founder World Bank)
Paul A. Samuelson
(economist)

SPORTS
Steve Davis *(snooker player)*
Bobby Fischer
(chess grand master)
Gary Kasparov
(chess grand master)
Sugar Ray Robinson *(boxer)*
Willie Shoemaker *(jockey)*

BAD DOGS
Hermann Goering
Adolf Hitler
Nicolò Machiavelli
Cardinal Jules Mazarin

and . . .
John Foster Dulles
(statesman)
Duke of Wellington
(soldier and politician)
Brigham Young
(Mormon Church)

OZOMATLI

•

Monkey

**Caring and sharing
an Aztec day sign of the West**

CHARACTERISTICS

VIRTUES	VICES
Artistic	Aloof
Charismatic	Dominating
Comedian	Drama queen
Creative	Eccentric
Entertainer	Indifferent
Graceful	Insecure
Leader	Manipulative
Musical	Mysterious
Romantic	Over-sexed
Sociable	Passionate
Teacher	

PERSONALITY

CALL IT bare-faced cheek, chutzpah, flamboyance, charisma or just style — whatever your taste in words, you're talking Aztec Ozomatli. This is Monkey language for the show man and woman, the entertainer and the teacher.

Take this modicum of Monkeys: suave Roger Moore, raunchy Tina Turner, exuberant Cab Calloway, strident Barbra Streisand, comic Harold Lloyd, and graceful Ginger Rogers — and you've encapsulated Monkey business.

Governed by Xochiplilli, the Aztec god of spring, flowers and dancing, this is the sign that brings us the highly strung, the excitable and the daring.

For many Monkeys, life is one grand stage on which to perform. And if they should choose a more selective audience, count yourself fortunate, or cursed, to be that audience, for a Monkey is part-clown, part-thespian.

There is also a weightier facet to Ozomatli. Herein can be found the comunicator-publishing magnate Alfred Knopf, the innovative scientist-Polaroid inventor Edwin Land, the painter Edgar Degas and the poet John Keats. You'll also find 'saints', like Helen Keller and a quota of sinners, like gangster Diamond Jim Brady and mass-murderer Charles Manson.

Some Monkeys were born to rule, like the founder of the Habsburg dynasty, Empress Maria Theresa, American Presidents James Madison and Ronald Reagan, British Prime Ministers Sir Edward Heath and Sir Harold Wilson, and French President Charles de Gaulle; others, like South Africa's Nelson Mandela, found power thrust upon them.

FAMOUS MONKEYS

INNOVATORS & ENTREPRENEURS
Jacques-Yves Cousteau
(underwater explorer)
Michael Faraday *(physicist)*
William Friese-Greene
(television)
Dr Edwin Land
(photography)
Gregor Mendel *(geneticist)*
Georg Simon Ohm
(physicist)
J.C. Penney *(trader)*
Jonas Salk *(physician)*
Rudolf Steiner
(educationalist)
Carl Zeiss *(optics)*

WRITERS
C.S. Forester
Walter de la Mare
John Keats
Arthur Koestler
Stanley Kubrick
John Le Carré
Doris Lessing
Joe Orton
Conrad Richter
Bram Stoker
Cesar Vallejo
Johann Wyss

ACTORS
Peter Cushing
Robert de Niro
Stewart Granger
Harold Lloyd
Roger Moore
Ginger Rogers

HEADS OF STATE & POLITICIANS
Charles de Gaulle
Sir Edward Heath
Chaim Herzog
James Madison
Nelson Mandela
Empress Maria Theresa
Ronald Reagan
Sir Harold Wilson

SINGERS & MUSICIANS
Count Basie
David Bowie
Cab Calloway
Ray Conniff
Stan Getz
Martha Reeves
Richard Strauss
Igor Stravinsky
Barbra Streisand
Tina Turner
Rudy Vallee
Efrem Zimbalist

NAUGHTY MONKEYS
Diamond Jim Brady
Patricia Hearst

BAD MONKEY
Charles Manson

and . . .
Edgar Degas *(artist)*
Grinling Gibbons
(woodcarver)
Helen Keller
*(handicapped author
and teacher)*
Alfred Knopf *(publisher)*
Joan Miró *(artist)*
Ernest Shepard
(children's book illustrator)
Johnny Weissmuller
(swimmer)

MALINALLI
·
Grass

**Sensitive and empathic
an Aztec day sign of the South**

CHARACTERISTICS

VIRTUES	VICES
Adorable	Bloodthirsty
Caring	Dictatorial
Compassionate	Dismissive
Creative	Ego-tripping
Entrancing	Gossipy
Musical	Malicious
Romantic	Manipulative
Sensitive	Materialistic
Thoughtful	Vindictive

PERSONALITY

HISTORICALLY, the ancient Aztecs thought of Grass as the sign of the penitent. Grass was used to draw blood from tongues and other body parts in ritual worship. This has been transformed in modern terms from penance to romance, with some of history's greatest lovers and artists being born under this sign.

Especially notable is the high number of Grass women who quickly rise to public prominence under the watchful eye of the Patecatl, the Mayan god of healing. Men who star under this sign are, like Casanova, adored or desired by women all over the world, either because they adore women, like the artist Jean Fragonard, or because they offer a unique appeal to the female senses, like volatile tennis-player John McEnroe.

Some Grass men can actually play a convincing female role (actor Robin Williams), sing timeless love songs, like Nat King Cole, or revel in gossip, like diarist Samuel Pepys.

However, history reveals that, of all the Aztec signs, Malinalli is the one offering women the chance to prove their creative worth. Some examples include singer Kathleen Ferrier and aviatrix Amelia Earhart, social commentator Emily Post, writers Jane Austen and Judith Krantz, and anthropologist Margaret Mead.

Curiously, those men who resent and resist the healing facet of Grass can become revolutionaries, like Lenin, Trotsky and Karl Marx. Yet some exploit their boyish charms – actors Jerry Lewis, Christopher Reeves and Eddie Murphy – or offer musical romanticism, like the composer Claude Debussy and performer Liberace.

But Grass is *not* a castrating sign for men: it offers power to those who wish it, for instance, J. Edgar Hoover, Dwight D. Eisenhower and Robert Kennedy. Masculine entrepreneurs have been born under this sign: Canadian press baron Lord Beaverbrook, the financier Baron Rothschild and German metallurgist Alfred Krupp were all men born under – but determined not to be put out to – Grass!

FAMOUS GRASSES

COMPOSERS
Claude Debussy
Maurice Ravel

WRITERS
Jane Austen
Lord Byron
O. Henry
Judith Krantz
Frederick Marryat
Guy de Maupassant
Samuel Pepys
Emily Post
Françoise Sagan
Richard Scarry
Robert Louis Stevenson
Count Leo Tolstoy

SPORTSMEN
Magic Johnson *(baseball)*
John McEnroe *(tennis)*
Daley Thompson
(decathalon)

REVOLUTIONARIES
Lenin
Karl Marx
Thomas Paine
Charles Stewart Parnell
Leon Trotsky

INNOVATORS & ENTREPRENEURS
Amelia Earhart
(aviatrix)
Alfred Krupp
(industrialist)
Antoine Laurent Lavoisier
(chemist)
Margaret Mead
(anthropologist)
Friedrich Wilhelm Nietzsche
(philosopher)
George M. Pullman
(industrialist)

STATESMEN
Dwight D. Eisenhower
Robert F. Kennedy
Juan Perón
Itzhak Rabin

ACTORS
Peter Finch
Glenn Ford
Stan Laurel
Gertrude Lawrence
Jerry Lewis
Eddie Murphy
Christopher Reeves
Spencer Tracy
Robin Williams

**SINGERS &
MUSICIANS**
Kate Bush
Enrico Caruso
Lou Christie
Eddie Cochran
Nat King Cole
Duane Eddy
Kathleen Ferrier
Mick Fleetwood
Peter Gabriel
Liberace
Dame Nellie Melba
Artie Shaw
Pete Townshend
Bert Weedon
Stevie Wonder

BAD GRASSES
Casanova
Marquis de Sade
Lee Harvey Oswald

and . . .
Lord Beaverbrook
(press baron)
Jean Honoré Fragonard
(artist)
J. Edgar Hoover *(FBI)*
Rudolf Nureyev
(ballet dancer)
Sir Carol Reed
(movie director)
Baron Rothschild
(financier)
George Stubbs *(artist)*
William Stukeley
(English antiquarian)

ACATL

·

Reed

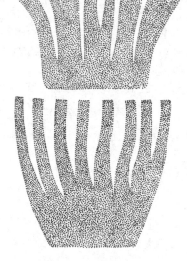

**Pioneers and motivators
an Aztec day sign of the East**

CHARACTERISTICS

VIRTUES	VICES
Accomplished	Aggressive
Ambitious	Destructive
Balanced	Dogmatic
Crusading	Dominating
Determined	Prima donna
Far-sighted	Shallow
Philosophical	Stubborn
Psychic	Unsettling
Quick-witted	Warring
Visionary	Wounding

PERSONALITY

THE AZTECS used reeds for making arrows and encouraged children born under this sign to develop their skills as warriors. More recent examples of Acatl-born people have shown no fears of launching into battle: notably the Chinese Chiang Kai-shek, the Israeli David Ben Gurion and the American President Franklin D. Roosevelt.

The Mayan deity linked to this sign was Tezcatlipoca, known as the Smoking Mirror and god of magic and time. Perhaps a contemporary reflection of this can be seen in the work of those Reed-born fathers of modern psychology, Sigmund Freud and Carl Jung. Other 'magical' Reeds were the famed French astrologer Nostradamus and theosophy founder Annie Besant.

This is a sign of accomplishment, of competence and of goal setting. There's also a pioneering flavour — as seen in the crusading work of contemporary consumer champion Ralph Nader.

Yet popularity seems to be a side issue for most of Acatl's sons and daughters. Their main thrust is towards achievement; even if this does bring reluctant acknowledgement from their enemies, the battle is undoubtedly secondary to the supreme goal.

The deeper levels of self-awareness that Reed offers its sons and daughters mean that they have little fear of others. Scorn washes over them, such is the depth of their personal convictions.

However, as the partners of Reeds will know, here is a sign that refuses to be locked in. And if for some reason Reeds are unable to indulge in their urgent need to travel in the physical body, then they will wander in the mind and bring us back the benefits of all this introspective searching in the form of books on philosophy, psychology or spiritual matters.

Another curiosity of this sign is that it contains some of the world's leading photographers, from the pioneering portraiture of the Victorian Julia Margaret Cameron to the fashion-conscious lenses of Irving Penn and Edward Steichen.

FAMOUS REEDS

MUSICIANS
Hector Berlioz
Johannes Brahms
Sir Charles Hallé
Otto Klemperer
Sir Yehudi Menuhin
Giacomo Puccini
Andrés Segovia

WRITERS
Walter de la Mare
Charles Dickens
Ralph Waldo Emerson
Graham Greene
Dashiell Hammett
Gerard Manley Hopkins
Aldous Huxley
Philip Larkin
D.H. Lawrence
Salman Rushdie
Lytton Strachey
Joseph Wambaugh
Evelyn Waugh
Thomas Wolfe
William Wordsworth

PHOTOGRAPHERS
Julia Margaret Cameron
Henri Cartier-Bresson
Irving Penn
Edward Steichen

SINGERS
Maria Callas
Roger Daltrey
Barbara Dickson
Judy Garland
Marvin Gaye
Eddy Grant
Mahalia Jackson
Billy J. Kramer
Joni Mitchell
Jimmy Osmond
Suzi Quatro
Andrew Ridgeley
Diana Ross
Neil Sedaka
Dame Kiri Te Kanawa
Dionne Warwick

INNOVATORS & ENTREPRENEURS
Karl Benz *(cars)*
Louis Blériot *(aviator)*
Annie Oakley
(markswoman)
William Paley *(broadcasting)*
Paul Revere
(US patriot and silversmith)
Henry Stiegel
(iron and glass master)
Louis Comfort Tiffany
(painter and glassmaker)

ACTORS
Dame Edith Evans
Mel Gibson
Kenneth More
Philip Schofield
Paul Scofield
Peter Ustinov
Caterina Valente
Dennis Waterman
Bruce Willis

STATESMEN & POLITICIANS
Menachem Begin
Chiang Kai-shek
David Ben Gurion
Dag Hammarskjöld
Nikita Khrushchev
Conor Cruise O'Brien
William Penn
Franklin D. Roosevelt
Hendrik F. Verwoerd

PSYCHOLOGY & THE SPIRITUAL
Annie Besant
Sigmund Freud
Carl Jung
Archbishop William Laud
Nostradamus

and . . .
Daniel Boone
Empress Joséphine de Beauharnais
(Napoleon's consort)
Jesse Jackson
Ralph Nader
Joe Namath *(sportsman)*
Mayer Amschel Rothschild *(banker)*
Peter Paul Rubens

OCELOTL

·

Ocelot

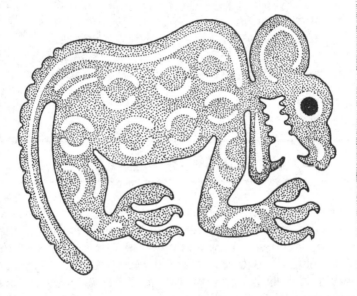

Mental and analytical
an Aztec day sign of the North

CHARACTERISTICS

VIRTUES	VICES
Athletic	Aggressive
Daring	Alcoholic
Determined	Complex
Generous	Deceptive
Graceful	Drug abuser
Humanitarian	Rebellious
Imaginative	Sarcastic
Leader	Tenacious
Pioneering	Warlike
Powerful	

PERSONALITY

POUNCE-POWER is perhaps the best way to describe the main virtue of those born under the Aztec sign of the Ocelot. This was — and is — one of the most fearless four-footed animals, a big cat that hunts with grace. The same applies to many of history's sons and daughers born centuries after the Aztecs were decimated.

Whether it be the feline grace of contemporary tennis champion Boris Becker, the beauty of prima ballerina Dame Margot Fonteyn or the hammer fist of World War Two, General George S. Patton, that instinctive sense of timing and rhythm is inborn.

Such was the reputation of the ocelot's ability to conceal itself that the Aztecs considered Ocelot-born to be natural spies — an ability highly prized within this warrior nation.

Another quality was this big cat's loyalty to its mate – a virtue much appreciated by the surprisingly puritanical Aztecs. Traditionally, this quality applies to those born under this sign: they are said to make excellent and faithful partners.

There is a competitive side to the Ocelot nature which can, at times, need careful handling. Negative Ocelots can indulge in the fantasy of illusion and self-deception – as seen in the life of Richard M. Nixon.

There can also be inherent natural cruelty, like the fanaticism of English General Oliver Cromwell. Sometimes this manifests in self-abuse, as in the larger-than-life style of Ernest Hemingway.

Many of today's Ocelots find fame prowling the world's pop festival stages, where they perform before appreciative thousands.

FAMOUS OCELOTS

MUSICIANS
Stephen Foster
Benny Goodman
Alan Jay Lerner
Felix Mendelssohn
Sviatoslav Richter
Sir Georg Solti

SINGERS
Phil Collins
Enya
Frankie Lane
Randy Newman
Cliff Richard
Keith Richards
Linda Ronstadt
Paul Simon
Connie Stevens
Bonnie Tyler
Luther Vandross
Kim Wilde

WRITERS
Emily Dickinson
Ernest Hemingway
Andrew Lang
John Masefield
Edna O'Brien
George Bernard Shaw

ACTORS
Leslie Howard
Patsy Kensit
Charles Laughton
Claude Rains
Arnold Schwarzenegger

SPORTSMEN
Boris Becker *(tennis)*
Fred Perry *(tennis)*
Emil Zatopek *(runner)*

POLITICIANS
James Keir Hardie
Andrew Jackson
Richard M. Nixon
Ian Smith
Margaret Thatcher
Lech Walesa

**PIONEERS &
ENTREPRENEURS**
Amelia Bloomer *(fashion)*
Martin Luther *(theologian)*
Sir Isaac Newton
(physicist)
Mungo Park *(explorer)*
John Smeaton
(civil engineer)
Benjamin Spock
(childcare expert)

CARS
Rudolf Diesel
Henry Ford
John de Lorean

and . . .
Oliver Cromwell
Dame Margot Fonteyn
Wild Bill Hickok
George S. Patton
Steven Spielberg

CUAUHTLI

•

Eagle

**Caring and sharing
an Aztec day sign of the West**

CHARACTERISTICS

VIRTUES	VICES
Artistic	Aggressive
Courageous	Complex
Creative	Dominating
Faithful	Escapist
Intellectual	Intolerant
Perceptive	Jealous
Philosophical	Rigid
Pioneering	Stubborn
Popular	Vain
Proud	Warlike

PERSONALITY

LIKE THE PREVIOUS SIGN, the Eagle is one of the Aztec warrior creatures, and people born under this sign were encouraged constantly to polish their battle skills. Just like this king of the birds, they were expected to be far-sighted and to be able to plan their strategies in great detail in the expectation of success. Something of this quality lingers in the list of contemporary Eagles. Those artists, writers, musicians and painters who have proved successful have gleaned something from the soaring vision of the Eagle-eyed, and the addition of stamina has enabled them to see their dreams materialize.

There's an element of perfectionism here, which can cause problems in relationships, because spouses can become 'widows' or 'widowers' to the obsessive cause of their Eagle mate.

Partners apart, the Eagle-born are solitary in their chosen field. Competition is not for them; rather the concept of challenging the self and spending lonely hours creating a masterpiece to meet its creator's high standards. The Eagle is so perceptive that he or she can spot the minutest detail, allowing readers, viewers or listeners to relax, confident in the knowledge that they are in the hands of a master or mistress, whatever their chosen skill.

Eagles are truly free spirits, with scant regard for rules and regulations; Errol Flynn and John Dillinger were both Eagle-born. And when Cuauhtli sets out to capture a mate, he or she will brook no opposition, as naval hero Lord Nelson discovered when Eagle-born Lady Emma Hamilton set her sights upon him.

This perception of the human condition can be turned towards helping us to laugh at ourselves, as proven by the humorous Eagle cartoonist, Jules Feiffer.

FAMOUS EAGLES

WRITERS
Anton Chekhov
C. Day-Lewis
Wilhelm Grimm
Georgette Heyer
Charles Kingsley
John Osborne
Dorothy Parker
Sir Terence Rattigan
Jean-Paul Sartre
Siegfried Sassoon
Gertrude Stein
Tom Stoppard
Harriet Beecher Stowe
Fay Weldon
Oscar Wilde
Emile Zola

MUSICIANS
Aaron Copland
Sir Edward Elgar
Stephen Sondheim
Sir William Walton

SPORTS
Jimmy Connors
(tennis)
Chris Evert
(tennis)
Katarina Witt
(athletics)

SINGERS
J.J. Cale
Woody Guthrie
Bill Haley
Gary Kemp
Dame Vera Lynn
Ricky Nelson
Jim Reeves
Sinitta
Ringo Starr

PIONEERS
Giambattista Bodoni
(typographer)
Wilhelm Conrad Roentgen
(physicist)
Marie Curie
(chemist)
M.C. Escher
(graphics)
Auguste Escoffier
(chef)
Leroy Grumman
(aviation)
Serge Lifar
(ballet)
Emanuel Swedenborg
(mystic)
Florenz Ziegfeld
(theatre producer)

ACTORS
Woody Allen
Ingrid Bergman
Albert Finney
Errol Flynn
Cary Grant
Dustin Hoffman
Sir Laurence Olivier
Kiefer Sutherland

STATESMEN
Sir Winston Churchill
Moshe Dyan
John F. Kennedy
Imre Nagy
(Hungarian prime minister)
Lester B. Pearson

and . . .
John Dillinger
Jules Feiffer
Lady Emma Hamilton

COZCAQUAUHTLI

·

Vulture

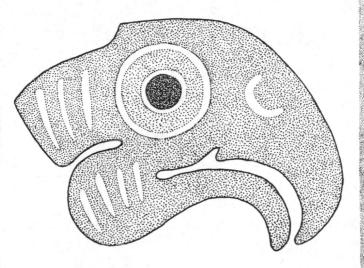

Sensitive and empathic
an Aztec day sign of the South

CHARACTERISTICS

VIRTUES	VICES
Determined	Blinkered
Exploratory	Cloying
Humanitarian	Dictatorial
Interpretive	Dogmatic
Inventive	Manipulative
Long-lived	Negative
Passionate	Obsessive
Pioneering	Rebellious
Wealthy	Sentimental

PERSONALITY

THE AZTECS believed that the Vulture-born experienced longevity, wealth — and nightmares: a curious combination more linked to their system of deities than the modern overview.

The link between ancient and modern lies in the key word *passion.* Cozcaquauhtli's sons and daughters have this driving force in abundance and — as always — they have the potential to employ this for positive or selfish motives. Positively, we have the passion of screenwriter Oliver Stone and such determined artists as Picasso and Cézanne, and the pioneering drive of a humanitarian like Lord Shaftesbury.

Here lies a driving force which, if harnessed to benefit humankind, can expand our frontiers of knowledge. Pioneering aviator Orville Wright, medical hero Sir Alexander

Fleming, automotive entrepreneurs Michelin and Goodyear, and the discoverer of modern photography, Joseph Niepce, have all contributed in this respect.

The down side is when such determination turns to obsession, even when the cause is just. World War Two hero, Swedish diplomat Raoul Wallenberg disappeared in mysterious circumstances while on a mission to save lives. Hollywood censor Will Hays made few friends in his determination to clean up celluloid imagery. Hitler's mistress, Eva Braun, lost her life in pursuit of her (and his) obsessions.

Vultures are high fliers who are familiar with the darker side of life. Some Vultures have made fame and fortune documenting this seamy side of human nature — mystery writer Ellery Queen demonstrates this well. Notable British author William Golding examined the negative side of adolescent boys in his novel *Lord of the Flies.* Canadian photographer Yousuf Karsh explored the harsh black-and-white extremes of film to create famous 'warts and all' portraits.

More recently, actor Michael Douglas gave a brilliant portrayal of the 'man in the street' driven beyond his limits when dealing with a stone-walling bureaucracy — the result demonstrates what happens when we suspend our normal value systems.

Vultures' preoccupation with the unknown often takes them into explored territory. Queen Victoria devoted much of her later life to consulting spiritualist mediums in attempts to contact her beloved German consort, Prince Albert. Writer Colin Wilson became both fascinated and fearful of the paranormal in his quest for esoteric knowledge.

FAMOUS VULTURES

MUSICIANS
Burt Bacharach
Percy Faith
George Gershwin
James Last
Gustav Mahler
Cole Porter
Dmitri Shostakovich
Jean Sibelius
Arturo Toscanini
Ralph Vaughan Williams

ARTISTS
Paul Cézanne
Pablo Picasso
Sir Joshua Reynolds
George Romney
Sir John Tenniel

ACTORS
Rowan Atkinson
Marlon Brando
Doris Day
Michael Douglas
Katharine Hepburn
Boris Karloff
Sir Harry Lauder
Debbie Reynolds
Henry Winkler

WRITERS
Ray Bradbury
Truman Capote
William Golding
Robert Graves
Marshall McLuhan
Marcel Proust
Ellery Queen
George Sand
Georges Simenon
Alexander Solzhenitsyn
Colin Wilson

SINGERS
Marc Bolan
Natalie Cole
Elvis Costello
Terence Trent D'Arby
Neil Diamond
Bob Dylan
Buddy Holly
Gladys Knight
Barry Manilow
Guy Mitchell
Van Morrison

EXPLORERS
James Cook
Sir Henry Morton Stanley

PIONEERS & INVENTORS

Sir Alexander Fleming
(penicillin)
Hans Wilhelm Geiger
(physicist)
Charles Goodyear *(tyres)*
Robert van de Graaff
(physicist)
Yousuf Karsh
(photographer)
William Thomson, Lord Kelvin
(physicist)
William H. Masters
(sexuality)
Edouard Michelin *(tyres)*
Edward R. Murrow
(broadcasting)
Joseph Nicéphore Niepce
(photography)
Walter Reed *(surgeon)*
Hermann Wilhelm Vogel
(chemist)
James Watt *(engineer)*
Sidney Webb
(social reformer)
Orville Wright *(aviator)*

STATESMEN & POLITICIANS

Lord Shaftesbury
Raoul Wallenberg
Casper Weinberger
Woodrow Wilson
Lee Kuan Yew
Andrew Young

and . . .

Eva Braun
Beau Brummell
Edgar Cayce
George Custer
Jack Dempsey
Will Hays
William Tecumseh Sherman
Oliver Stone
Studs Terkel
Queen Victoria

OLLIN
·
Earthquake

**Pioneers and motivators
an Aztec day sign of the East**

CHARACTERISTICS

VIRTUES	VICES
Charitable	Arrogant
Creative	Cunning
Exploring	Deceptive
Extrovert	Dismissive
Humanitarian	Domineering
Interpretive	Manipulative
Inventive	Persecuting
Pioneering	Power crazy
Statesmanlike	Unstable

PERSONALITY

JUST AS the ancient Aztec name would suggest, here are the people who have the proven ability to make the earth move. These folk have an instinctive knack of having their fingers on the public pulse and can feed back social trends to bring joy (or pain) to a mass audience.

The Earthquake-born dream their dreams in both Technicolor and Cinemascope and think only in terms of the world's biggest stages; not for them the cramped conditions of a local community hall: their venues must be international – or not at all.

Think *Gone with the Wind* and you are talking of the Earthquake David O. Selznick. Think South Africa and you are talking of Cecil Rhodes. Think dynasties and you are talking of the Shah of Iran. Think swashbuckle and you can only mean

Douglas Fairbanks Sr. And so it goes on, each of these earth movers needing the biggest canvas on which to paint their dreams.

Want to talk American presidents? Then look to the sons of Ollin to produce names like Thomas Jefferson, Theodore Roosevelt, Jimmy Carter and would-be, Michael Dukakis — all men unafraid of grasping the reins of power, where many a lesser mortal would fear to tread.

Who else but Rudolph Valentino could capture the hearts of millions of women with that smouldering intensity that seems so often to be a hallmark of the Earthquake-born? Who else but blockbuster novelist Arthur Hailey could contemplate tackling such broad plots? And who else but manager Brian Epstein could bring us the tonal range of The Beatles?

But when Earthquakes like Senator Joe McCarthy, Nazi SS boss Heinrich Himmler and his English fan Sir Oswald Mosley turn their public manipulation to the brutal side of life, it is time to emigrate.

Some Ollin-born are feared by the corporate world of vested interest. The astonishing inventions of former Yugoslavian Nikola Tesla (who discovered amazing ways of harnessing cheap electricity) were — according to many — suppressed as being too revolutionary.

FAMOUS EARTHQUAKES

LEADERS & HEADS OF STATE
Jimmy Carter
Dalai Lama
Thomas Jefferson
Cecil Rhodes
Theodore Roosevelt
Shah of Iran

POLITICIANS
Benjamin Franklin
Willy Brandt
Michael Dukakis
Joe McCarthy

ACTORS
Kim Basinger
Douglas Fairbanks Sr
Michael J. Fox
Larry Hagman
Lillie Langtry
Shirley Temple
Dame Ellen Terry
Rudolph Valentino

ARTISTS
Benvenuto Cellini
Marc Chagall
Henri de Toulouse-Lautrec
Joseph M.W. Turner

MUSICIANS
Acker Bilk
Jimmy Dorsey
Arthur Rubinstein
Arnold Schoenberg
Antonio Vivaldi

TV & MOVIES
Jackie Gleason
Jean-Luc Godard
Alfred Hitchcock
Stanley Kramer
Sydney Pollack
David O. Selznick

WRITERS
Sir James Barrie
Brendan Behan
A.J. Cronin
Antoine de Saint-Exupéry
Henry Fielding
Arthur Hailey
P.D. James
Dr Samuel Johnson
H.P. Lovecraft
Harold Pinter
J.D. Salinger
Edgar Wallace
Morris L. West

SINGERS
Chris de Burgh
Carole King
Dolly Parton
Tommy Steele
Hank Williams

PIONEERS & INNOVATORS
Gerardus Mercator
(cartogapher)
Nikola Tesla
(electrical engineer)
Linus Yale
(locksmith)

SHOCKING EARTHQUAKES
Georges Jacques Danton
Heinrich Himmler
Sir Oswald Mosley

and . . .
Brian Epstein
(record manager)
Ira Gershwin
(songwriter)
Sir Edmund Hillary
(mountaineer)
Harry Houdini
(escapologist)
Dorothea Lange
(photographer)
Rod Laver *(tennis)*

TECPATL
·
Knife

Mental and analytical
an Aztec day sign of the North

CHARACTERISTICS

VIRTUES	VICES
Bold	Accident-prone
Brave	Domineering
Courageous	Insecure
Creative	Intense
Crusading	Jealous
Determined	Self-absorbed
Inspired	Vain
Perceptive	Vindictive
Pioneering	Warlike
Valiant	
Wealthy	

PERSONALITY

TECPATL actually meant flint knife to the Aztecs. An esssential tool for every warrior and priest, it was used not only for sacrificial purposes but for making fire. It represented people who were 'sharp' or clever.

Our survey of contemporary Aztec Knives not only reflects this skill, but adds others. In modern terms, these are the people who are at the cutting edge of their respective fields. There are warriors who lived by the sword (Napoleon and Wild West hero Kit Carson); there are sportswomen who have won fame on their blades (ice-skaters Sonja Henie and Dorothy Hamill); artists who use a palette knife (Seurat and Grandma Moses); and authors who cut through acres of

verbiage to give us keen truths (Rudyard Kipling and columnist Hedda Hopper).

One overview suggests that the Aztec Knife-born have the choice of using their skills or of being used by others. There is analytical skill here (the French Cardinal Richelieu) and also the knife-edge of diplomacy (King Hussein of Jordan) and an understanding of the paranoid world of spies (author Len Deighton).

Some of the Tecpatl-born successfully trade their knives for other tools, like the conductor's baton of Glenn Miller or the general's baton of World War Two hero Douglas MacArthur. Others prefer microchips, like electronics genius Sir Clive Sinclair, or embrace the concept that the pen is mightier than the sword, like crusading *New York Times* publisher George Jones.

The penetrating insights of psychology also seem to appeal to the Knife-born. Here you will find experimental or pioneering practitioners, like Jean Piaget and the Gestalt founder Max Wertheimer. Above all, Knife is a sign of mental capacity and communications, the ability to précis and sub-edit. All of its sons and daughters have this skill and they choose how best to employ it.

FAMOUS KNIVES

MUSICIANS
Sir Adrian Boult
Hoagy Carmichael
Scott Joplin
Glenn Miller
Camille Saint-Saëns

LEADING LADIES
Jacqueline Kennedy
Eleanor Roosevelt

WILD WEST
Kit Carson
Wyatt Earp

WRITERS
Len Deighton
Fyodor Dostoievsky
George Eliot
Erle Stanley Gardner
William Hazlitt
Hedda Hopper
George Jones
Stephen King
Rudyard Kipling
Ogden Nash
Norman Vincent Peale
Alfred, Lord Tennyson
J.R.R. Tolkien
Leon Uris
Jules Verne

ARTISTS
Albrecht Dürer
Grandma Moses
Sidney Nolan
Georges Seurat

SINGERS
Harry Belafonte
Cher
Perry Como
Randy Crawford
Lonnie Donegan
Bob Geldof
George Harrison
Mark Knopfler
Keith Moon
Johnny Nash
Olivia Newton-John
Elizabeth Schwarzkopf
Suzanne Vega
Pete Waterman

ACTORS
Sir Charles Chaplin
James Dean
Lorne Greene
Don Johnson
Carole Lombard
Sophia Loren
Marcel Marceau
Gordon McCrae

MOVIE-MAKERS
Francis Ford Coppola
Martin Scorsese

HEADS OF STATE
Alexander Dubček
King Hussein of Jordan
Lyndon B. Johnson
Napoleon
Jawaharlal Nehru
Pope Pius lll

PIONEERS & ENTREPRENEURS
Walter Percy Chrysler *(cars)*
John Dunlop *(tyres)*
Sir John Herschel
(astronomer)
Ferdinand de Lesseps
(civil engineer)

Charles Macintosh *(chemist)*
Jean Piaget *(psychologist)*
Sir Clive Sinclair *(electronics)*
Sir Basil Spence *(architect)*
Manfred von Richthofen
(fighter pilot)
Max Wertheimer
(psychologist)

SPORTS
Dorothy Hamill *(skater)*
Sonja Henie *(skater)*
Ivan Lendl *(tennis)*

and . . .
Douglas MacArthur
Dan Quayle
Cardinal Richelieu
Ed Sullivan *(broadcaster)*
Pancho Villa

QUIAHUITL

·

Rain

**Caring and sharing
an Aztec day sign of the West**

CHARACTERISTICS

VIRTUES	VICES
Caring	Gullible
Childlike	Indulgent
Comforting	Outbursts
Compassionate	Perfectionist
Homemaking	Selfish
Innocent	Unsociable
Lucky	Unstable
Multifaceted	Victim
Peaceful	
Reassuring	

PERSONALITY

THE ANCIENT AZTECS saw Rain as one of their lucky signs. It was ruled by the hearth-fire goddess Chantico, and Mayan *advinos* (astrologers) would advise parents that the only thing they need fear about their Rain-born was that this particular goddess sometimes turned from providing a cosy hearth fire to the raging fury of a volcanic erruption. However, for the most part, these sons and daughters of Quiahuitl led a charmed and peaceful life.

A review of modern Rain folk endorses this ancient observation. Many of them have tried to bring us comfort and reassurance, especially in times of trouble. Hollywood gave us those reassuring heroes John Wayne, Jimmy Stewart and Henry Fonda, whose frequent roles as the ordinary guys defending their citizen's rights brought comfort to many.

This aspect is also clearly seen in the number of popular singers who have become household names. The soothing sounds of Pearl Bailey are just as timeless as the work of Leonard Cohen, Sting, Roy Orbison and even Meatloaf. Social reform is another instinctive objective of the Rain-born. Singer-songwriters Bob Seger and Pete Seeger reflect these urges to change society.

There is an effervescent youth factor to Rain folk. Millions of children have listened to the bedtime stories of Jacob Grimm and Dr Seuss, while older Rain-born have that eternal childlike curiosity that many find endearing.

This same youthful outlook can express itself successfully in comedy, as seen in the work of entertainers like Lenny Bruce and Peter Sellers, whose movie role as Chauncey Gardner in *Being There* reflected an innocence that entranced a nation.

Compassion is a major virtue in the armoury of Rain folk. Princess Diana reveals this in her concern for charities and the underprivileged.

FAMOUS RAIN MAKERS

SINGERS
Pearl Bailey
Leonard Cohen
Sacha Distel
Donovan
Billy Eckstine
Georgie Fame
Billy Fury
Janet Jackson
Annie Lennox
Little Richard
John McCormack
Meatloaf
Roy Orbison
Prince
Pete Seeger
Bob Seger
Sting
Toyah

MUSICIANS
Antonín Dvořák
Niccolo Paganini
Nelson Riddle
Ravi Shankar

FILM & TELEVISION
John Leslie Hyatt
Sidney Lumet
Ted Turner
Raoul Walsh

ACTORS
Sarah Bernhardt
Charles Bronson
Lon Chaney
Henry Fonda
Stanley Holloway
Kris Kristofferson
James Mason
Melina Mercouri
River Phoenix
James Stewart
John Wayne

WRITERS
Raymond Chandler
John Creasey
Jacob Grimm
Edgar Allan Poe
Dr Seuss
Mickey Spillane
Rex Stout
Jacqueline Susann

ARTISTS
Franz Hals
Paul Klee
Walter Sickert

JOURNALISTS
Joseph Pulitzer
Baron von Reuter
Walter Winchell

**HEADS OF STATE &
POLITICIANS**
Stanley Baldwin
Indira Gandhi
Maximilien Robespierre

**PIONEERS &
ENTREPRENEURS**
Karl Baedeker
(cartographer)
David Livingstone *(explorer)*
Sir Joseph Lockyer
(astronomer)
Sir Napier Shaw
(meteorologist)
Beatrice Webb
(social reformer)
Josiah Wedgwood *(potter)*

COMEDIANS
Lenny Bruce
Peter Sellers

**PSYCHOLOGY &
MYSTICISM**
Helena Blavatsky
(Russian theosophist)
Erich Fromm
Ivan Petrovich Pavlov

and . . .
Coco Chanel
Princess Diana
Bat Masterson
Auguste Rodin
Antoinette Sibley
Archbishop Desmond Tutu

XOCHITL

•

Flower

**Sensitive and empathic
an Aztec day sign of the South**

CHARACTERISTICS

VIRTUES	VICES
Artistic	Ambitious
Beautiful	Fanatical
Calm	Highly sexed
Creative	Insecure
Crusading	Materialistic
Graceful	Opportunistic
Idealistic	Self-centred
Musical	Tortured
Soothing	Unstable
Strong	
Talented	

PERSONALITY

THE LAST OF the Aztec day signs and one reserved for beautiful people. The Mayan goddess who rules them is Xochiquetzal, bringer of good fortune. Reported to make excellent partners with a natural *joie de vivre* and infectious happiness, this is the Aztec sign that celebrates some of history's most graceful (Grace Kelly and Deborah Kerr) and most intelligent (Albert Schweitzer and Albert Einstein) people.

Here are to be found the idealists, the crusaders and the world changers. Peace is their goal (Alfred Nobel) and change is their target (Mikhail Gorbachev and Boris Yeltsin). Yet some of these Flower children find cause to twist these humanitarian aims to more selfish ends (like the celebrated would-be British Parliamentary arsonist Guy Fawkes) or

plunge into the dark side of life, as seen in the tormented visions of William Blake.

Here is a sign for singers with the gift of touching and interpreting the needs of the public pulse; household names like Bing Crosby, Bruce Springsteen, Ray Charles and Karen Carpenter can be found in the list of famous Flower vocalists.

Sometimes this instinctive need to give can create deep anxieties within the souls of these peace-loving folk, especially if they lack adequate grounding. In extreme cases, this self-torture can manifest tragically (Karen Carpenter).

But for most Flower children there is sweetness and light, both within and without, to delight family, friends and often the world. This is a sign of creativity, artistic abilities and the skill to display them. The only danger comes when the element of perfectionism gets out of hand. It is for this reason that relationships based upon impossible dreams and illusions can be a stumbling block for some of these Flower people.

One classic example of the Flower ability to bring us the cosy reassurance of support for family values lies in the work of celebrated American artist Norman Rockwell, whose small-town images still convey and encapsulate the American Dream for many.

There are exceptions to the rule that says Flowerfolk are all perfect human beings. Just like each of the other Aztec signs, this one also has its scoundrels and scandal makers — people like Roman Polanski, the unashamed Nell Gwyn and the Prime Ministerial philanderer David Lloyd George. But for most Flower children, their role is to soothe and offer support. And they do this brilliantly.

FAMOUS FLOWERS

STATESMEN & POLITICIANS
Gerald Ford
Mikhail Gorbachev
David Lloyd George
Sir Robert Menzies
François Mitterrand
Emperor Haile Selassie
Boris Yeltsin

MOVIES
Sir Alexander Korda
Sam Peckinpah
Roman Polanski
Franco Zeffirelli

SINGERS
Rick Astley
Karen Carpenter
Ray Charles
Bing Crosby
Bobby Darin
Fats Domino
Gloria Estefan
Phil Everly
John Lee Hooker
Gene Pitney
Sandie Shaw
Bruce Springsteen
Hank Williams

THEATRE
Sir Peter Hall
Konstantin Stanislavsky

ACTORS
James Cagney
Fernandel
Charlton Heston
Deborah Kerr
Basil Rathbone
Sir Ralph Richardson
William Shatner
Patrick Swayze
Dame Sybil Thorndike

WRITERS
William Blake
Herman Hesse
Patricia Highsmith
Victor Hugo
Henry Robinson Luce
S.S. McClure
Henry Rider Haggard
Mary Shelley
Gloria Steinem
Tom Wolfe

SPORTS
Jack Kramer *(tennis)*
Jessie Owens *(athletics)*
Mark Spitz *(swimming)*

ARTISTS
Francisco Goya
Henri Matisse
Norman Rockwell
Sir Anthony Van Dyck
Vincent van Gogh

and . . .
Clarence Darrow
Mary Baker Eddy
Albert Einstein
Guy Fawkes
Princess Grace of Monaco
Nell Gwyn
Alfred Nobel
Albert Schweitzer
William Henry Vanderbilt

Bibliography

———————●———————

The Maya by Michael Coe (Thames & Hudson, 1966)

Magic from Mexico by Mary Devine (Llewellyn, 1982)

What Became of the Mayans? by Pamela Francis (Pergamon, 1969)

The Ancient Civilisations of Peru by J. Alden Mason (Pelican, 1957)

Secrets of Mayan Science/Religion by Hunbatz Men (Bear & Co, 1989)

The Anatomy of an Andean Myth: The History of a Cosmology by William F. Sullivan (unpublished thesis for the University of St Andrews, Scotland)

Aztec Astrology by K.C. Tunnicliffe (L.N. Fowler, 1979)

The Story of Fulfilled Prophecy by Justine Glass (Cassell, 1969)

Index

●